THE HOUSE OF LIGHT

ORO Editions
Publishers of Architecture, Art, and Design
Gordon Goff: Publisher

www.oroeditions.com
info@oroeditions.com

Published by ORO Editions

Text by Erik Dyar
Book Design by Takigawa Design with Jay Galster
Edited by Eric Brown
Managing Editor: Jake Anderson

10 9 8 7 6 5 4 3 2 1 First Edition

ISBN: 978-1-951541-14-9

Color Separations and Printing: ORO Group Ltd.
Printed in China.

ORO Editions makes a continuous effort to minimize the overall carbon footprint of its publications. As part of this goal, ORO Editions, in association with Global ReLeaf, arranges to plant trees to replace those used in the manufacturing of the paper produced for its books. Global ReLeaf is an international campaign run by American Forests, one of the world's oldest nonprofit conservation organizations. Global ReLeaf is American Forests' education and action program that helps individuals, organizations, agencies, and corporations improve the local and global environment by planting and caring for trees.

THE HOUSE OF LIGHT

ERIK DYAR

ORO EDITIONS

FOREWORD

This is a story about a house . . . a home . . . a construction project . . . a work of architecture. It chronicles what happened, and what resulted, when John Thodos—an architect of extraordinary vision who spent a long, distinguished career refining his unique architectural language—came together with Peter and Kay Nosler to create a House of Light. These were clients who respected his vision but had particular needs of their own.

Driving the design and construction teams to do their best work with the highest standards of craftsmanship, the Noslers fearlessly challenged the norms of their conventional residential neighborhood in Menlo Park, California. The formidable statement of Modern design that resulted in 625 Hobart Street wasn't what Kay and Peter would have envisioned for themselves years before. As happily married empty nesters, they had previously called "home" a more traditional two-story house directly across the street from what would become their unconventional new residence.

But Kay Nosler's diagnosis with a rare neurological disorder in 2004 became a catalyst for the project. Her medical condition was a primary driver of the design, but her insistence on getting the very best from her architect was key to the exceptional results. In many ways the new home also symbolized Peter and Kay's love. The experience of designing and building their new house would take them on a journey from a general skepticism of Contemporary architecture to a genuine love for it.

Peter, who helped found one of the nation's leading construction companies that started in the Bay area, was also no ordinary homeowner. His passion for construction technology and craft—along with playing an active role in the design and construction of the new home—were instrumental throughout the process.

The final work of architect John Thodos, the Nosler House is infused with the refinements of ideas he had been cultivating throughout his career. With the support of Peter, along with general contractor Greg Marrone and his team, John was able to manifest his architectural vision in an uncompromising way.

Although I had founded my own firm, DYAR Architecture, by the time John started designing 625 Hobart Street, I returned to work with him solely on this magnificent project. To describe him as just a mentor would not do our relationship justice. He first introduced me to the world of architecture when I was a nine-year-old boy, at which time he began dating my mother for five years. By age 18, I was working in his office during the summer and continued doing so throughout my years in architecture school. Upon graduating from the University of Oregon, John's alma mater, he invited me to work for him in Carmel-by-the-Sea, California, where he had permanently relocated. For the next 17 years, I worked by his side as his primary associate on all of his most significant projects.

Erik Dyar and John Thodos at John's Torres Street House in Carmel (2009).

This experience perhaps gave me singular insight into his work and life. John was a friend, boss, father, and mentor. He was one of the most important people in my life—and certainly the most influential one. John taught me to love architecture and life with a passion, and it was my love and respect for him and his work that kept me by his side for so long. To be with John again and help create this one-of-a-kind home was a blessing. Working with him alongside Peter, Kay, Greg, and the team was an inspiration that will stay with me forever.

We wanted to tell the story of the visionary people who joined forces to create this unique home, of its design and construction process, and of the house itself and how it lives today in a quiet Menlo Park neighborhood. And now we invite you to join us on an inspiring journey of the heart and imagination that illuminated the way for the House of Light.

—Erik Dyar

OWNERS' STORY

Peter and Kay with their son Zander shortly after he graduated from Stanford University.

Despite the powerful and unique architectural form that confronts the passerby at 625 Hobart Street, this was not a design that came preconceived from the individual mind of the artist/architect. The conception for the House of Light was inextricably tied to the two people who called it home. To see how and why Peter and Kay Nosler put considerable efforts and resources into building this Contemporary piece of architecture, one has to understand the path their lives took. Their journey, and the story of their home's creation, is intellectual, artistic, and emotional.

FIRST HOMES

The general location of the Noslers' first custom-built residence was never really in doubt. Menlo Park had long been "home" for the couple. In 1975 they had purchased their first house just west of downtown. It was a relatively humble two-bedroom, one-bath single-story structure in what Peter describes as the "California Ordinary" style. With Peter in the construction industry, remodeling and adding to the home were a natural progression, especially with a young son to raise. Over the years, the Noslers built onto the house twice, learning to adapt it to accommodate their needs, lifestyle, and tastes.

In 1990, the Noslers decided to move to a new home designed just for them. They found a nice lot in another quiet, residential Menlo Park neighborhood: 620 Hobart Street, which became the site of the first of two homes they would build on this street. Located between busy Santa Cruz and Middle Avenues, this is one of the longer, uninterrupted blocks in this small, tree-lined city in the San Francisco Bay Area. It was to become what Peter termed "our street" for the next quarter century.

620 Hobart Street, soon after its completion in 1995.

The Noslers hired an architect (not John Thodos, whom they had yet to meet) and embarked upon a rigorous design process, balancing their needs and ambitions with what they could afford. Clearly they had progressed beyond planning mere additions or remodels to thinking deeply about function and how space related to the way they lived. They had also grown to love the Craftsman style of architecture, with its overhanging roofs, shingles, and warm-wood detailing, and so they chose it for their 620 Hobart Street house.

A JOURNEY TO MODERNISM

While it's true that the Noslers were still more comfortable with a Traditional architectural style, their transition to Contemporary had already begun. Peter recalls when he and Kay visited Paris in 1982 and saw the Centre Georges Pompidou for the first time. Designed by then-partners Richard Rogers and Renzo Piano, the Centre was completed in 1977. The Noslers were impressed by how this raw exoskeleton of a building—with its exposed ductwork and structure, an unapologetic monument to the Contemporary age—could work in such a complementary way with the classical old buildings that surrounded it. They were fascinated by the Centre's overall look, and Peter was especially drawn to its advanced construction techniques.

Captivated by its architectural innovations, Peter and Kay visited Centre Pompidou many times.

At about this same time, the Noslers had joined the Contemporary Collectors Circle (CCC) at Stanford University's Cantor Arts Center, and began traveling with the group around the world. The CCC focused on Modern and Contemporary art and architecture. As the Noslers spent more time contemplating Contemporary art at museums, as well as visiting collectors' homes and some notable studios, they began buying pieces for their home. One of their first significant purchases was "Head," a painting by Jerry McLaughlin that was some five-feet square. This acquisition marked a major step for the Noslers into the world of Contemporary art and design. And their progress was significantly enriched when, during a subsequent trip to Paris, they visited Le Corbusier's Villa Savoye and Alvar Aalto's Maison Louis Carré.

No doubt an important component of what united this couple was their shared curiosity of the world and a love of learning. They spent significant time together enjoying the discovery of new places, new ideas, new art, and new architecture. Beyond anything else, perhaps this steady current of curiosity led them to bring their 625 Hobart Street home—the House of Light—to fruition.

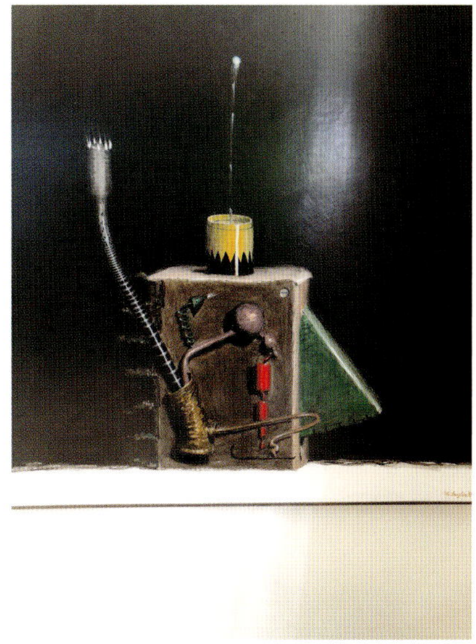

Jerry McLaughlin's painting, "Head," started the Noslers' dedicated acquisition program of art while they lived at 620 Hobart Street.

BUILDING A CAREER

College majors in math and physics, followed by graduate school in biophysics, marked a pathway to a teaching career for Peter. But having developed a passion for building and cabinetry in his early youth, he couldn't resist the opportunity to follow his heart—rather than what he felt was the misguided belief of his parents, who expected him to follow his grandparents into a lifelong teaching career.

Peter spent a number of years moving up the ranks in a major Bay Area construction firm. Then in 1990, Kay urged him to join two of his fellow managers in starting their own business, DPR Construction, which was named for the three partners: Doug, Peter, and Ron. Kay's support for DPR's success never wavered.

DPR grew into a most unusual firm. With some twenty offices and more than five-thousand employees, the size and reach were impressive. But the partners' true achievement was a unique building process that made complex projects a reality for their customers. Whether envisioning hospitals, research labs, data centers, or office and campus buildings, the innovative owner-architect-contractor team concept that DPR pioneered was highly successful. The firm has constructed notable properties and worked with leading architects. Peter himself was deeply involved with projects such as the San Francisco Asian Art Museum, in collaboration with Gae Aulenti; and Pixar Studios, working directly with Steve Jobs and Peter Bohlin of Bohlin Cywinski Jackson Architects, among many others.

DPR Construction grew into one of the nation's leading constructor of hospitals and other technical projects. Sutter Hospital in Castro Valley, California, is an early example of DPR's landmark Integrated Project Delivery (IPD) approach.

Such associations undoubtedly increased Peter's appreciation of Contemporary architecture, while his vast construction experience and considerable skills gave him the confidence to later pursue John Thodos' architectural vision at 625 Hobart Street. Peter's experience working with an extensive array of personalities and talents (not to mention huge egos) also likely contributed to what may well be his most impressive skill: getting the best from people on a project and motivating them as a team to achieve a common goal. This is no small feat, whether applied to a multi-billion-dollar construction company or to a group of diverse people building a rather unique single-family house.

Kay, often with Peter in tow, frequented quilt shows and fabric shops. Many of her quilts, such as this one, were gifts to family and friends.

KAY FINDS HER OWN CALLING

Around the time that DPR was founded, Kay began making quilts and produced some forty of them that earned her a reputation as a master quilt maker. Whereas Peter became a very competent cabinetmaker at a young age, Kay took up quilting much later in life, having worked in medical records and subsequently for one of the Saga founders. When the Noslers became empty nesters, she grew quite serious about advancing her quilting skills and acquiring unique fabrics. Colorful Kaffe Fassett designs were something she treasured. And while she rarely strayed from rectilinear designs, there was definitely a Contemporary style to her quilts.

MEETING JOHN THODOS

The Noslers met John Thodos about midway along their journey to embracing the Contemporary style. In the 1980s they had purchased an old bungalow in the Central California village of Carmel-by-the-Sea. It was a small lot with a rather simple, humble structure. It also had charm and character, and was just three blocks from beautiful Carmel Beach. Periodically the Noslers would escape the bustling San Francisco Bay Area to spend time in their "tuckaway" (Carmel has no numbered street addresses, so houses have names). They took many walks and enjoyed looking at the houses, particularly newer structures. One stood out to them: a modern wood and glass home on Scenic Drive, the street that borders the beach. This turned out to be the residence of John Thodos, a well-known local architect.

Ten years later, the Noslers decided their now-decaying "Carmel charmer" needed to be replaced with a new house. They interviewed three local architects, including John Thodos. Both Peter and Kay appreciated the Scenic Drive house and other contemporary examples of Thodos' work. However, Kay loved the character of the original cottage and had considered replacing it with a new structure with a similar feel. John didn't help his case to get the job when he began his interview by saying, "I don't do bungalows." Peter thought that using a slightly different term might appeal to John's sensibilities and help bring this architect onboard. He assured John that he and Kay appreciated John's approach to modern architecture, and that they would welcome a "Contemporary bungalow." This made John feel much better. So, combined with how much he liked and enjoyed this charming couple, John agreed to design their new Carmel home.

Their partnership, the first of two—this one in Carmel, the other later in Menlo Park, on the House of Light—worked splendidly. John was happy to design a simple but minimal exterior using traditional raw forms that suited Kay's desire for "Carmel cottage character," while he worked with Peter on more modern detailing for the interior. The collaboration went smoothly and everyone was pleased with the final result. With the house completed, the Noslers had no plans for another project, but had become friends with John and his wife, Judy.

A NEW HOME

What tragically became the strongest impetus for building the Nosler House occurred in 2004. Kay, a healthy, active woman most of her life, suddenly showed her first symptoms of a serious neurological disorder. It was initially diagnosed as Parkinson's disease, which can take many years to become significantly debilitating. Sadly, Kay's illness progressed more quickly, and she appeared to be headed for life in a wheelchair. The Noslers realized their current two-story residence wasn't working and that they needed a house on one level providing complete accessibility for a wheelchair-bound resident. But Menlo Park's Hobart Street was HOME, and Kay was adamant not to leave it. Never one to have made demands, she was bravely looking at a scary prognosis and didn't need to deal with moving to a strange new neighborhood on top of battling her health.

As they faced this realization, as if by magic, a small old house directly across from 620 Hobart Street suddenly became available, at #625. Peter jumped at the opportunity, and within days they were able to purchase the property. The Noslers didn't know what the future would hold, but they knew there was no time to waste. They needed a new home. It had to be designed to make Kay's newfound condition the best it could be—to make her life within its walls easy and fulfilling.

The process of creating the House of Light would need to be rewarding as well. It was becoming clear that every moment was precious, and both Kay and Peter sought to become deeply involved. An act of fate may have been the catalyst, but there was joy in embarking on this new creative process, which they saw as a culmination of a shared, decades-long path of learning and discovery. There was nothing left to lose, nothing to hold back. From their travels and long, successful partnership, they knew what could be possible. They decided that this time, the home they wanted would be Contemporary and Modern: a piece of architecture that also functioned as a living work of art.

THE ARCHITECT'S STORY

The architecture of the late John Thodos, Fellow of the American Institute of Arts (FAIA), is one of synthesized influences that he refined into something new and unique. Thodos was a Greek American born in Chicago in 1934 and raised in Portland, Oregon. He was educated at the University of Oregon in Eugene, attending from 1955 through 1960, when the school thoroughly embraced the Modern movement and the work of the 20th-century masters of the International style—led by luminaries such as Mies van der Rohe and Le Corbusier, as well as the legendary Finnish master Alvar Aalto.

John grew up in the architectural milieu of the Pacific Northwest and what is now termed the "Northwest Regional" style, as practiced by John Yeon, Pietro Belluschi, and Van Evera Bailey, its key proponents. This style can be seen as what later became known as "Critical Regionalism," which interprets International-style Modernism through the climate and culture of a particular location. Key characteristics of the Northwest Regional style are the use of more humanizing, warm surfaces like wood siding (usually vertical), and a strong connection to garden and landscape, all of which came to be incorporated into John's architecture.

BRINGING WARMTH TO MODERNISM

Like Scandinavia, Portland can be cold and rainy. In both places we see the use of warm, natural materials to humanize spaces, along with expanses of glass to bring in needed sunlight, elements also seen in Aalto's work. "Warm Modernism" may sound like a term implying some sort of compromised

version of Modernism, yet here it simply refers to the use of materials and color palettes that are generated as responses to a regional climate and material availability, rather than as a purely aesthetic choice. John Thodos often described his version of the style as "Modern Humanism."

As a first-generation Greek American, John always felt strong ties to the "mother" country and Things Greek. After graduating from architecture school in 1960, he decided to see the country of his parents' birth for himself and took a six-month journey. Like Aalto, Le Corbusier, and other architects before him, this voyage influenced his own style. The traditional cubical white architecture of the Cyclades Islands held a particular power for him. These mostly flat-roof structures, their forms plastic and sharply carved elements in space, allow natural light to create a play of shadows on their surfaces and etch them out against the sky. These traditional buildings typically have deep openings that provide mystery inside, whose main spaces are augmented with niches. John incorporated these elements into the architectural themes that he would develop and refine throughout his career.

The David Eyre House in Portland, by Van Evera Bailey (1948), exhibits elements of the Northwest Regional Style—the architectural milieu that influenced John Thodos.

Interior of the Swan House in Portland, by John Yeon (1953), showing the use of "warm" materials in a modern space.

THE SPINE

To highlight the themes in the work of John Thodos, first one must consider the spine. So many of his buildings utilize this organizing principle. For John, it was all about expressing human movement with form and creating a magnificent space for it. If circulation is a form itself, then adjoining spaces don't necessarily have to be directly connected, thus opening more sides to natural light. The spine also is an "urban" idea, creating a street at the scale of a building. As with the Nosler House, John often included skylights to give even more sense of an outdoor street while adding the drama of the play of light throughout the day, directly connecting the inhabitants to Nature's clock.

A village on the Cyclades Islands of Greece with interlocking cubical forms cascading down the hillside.

Left: Top view of model of Thodos-designed "Gallery House" built in the Carmel Highlands, an earlier example of the "spine" in John's work.

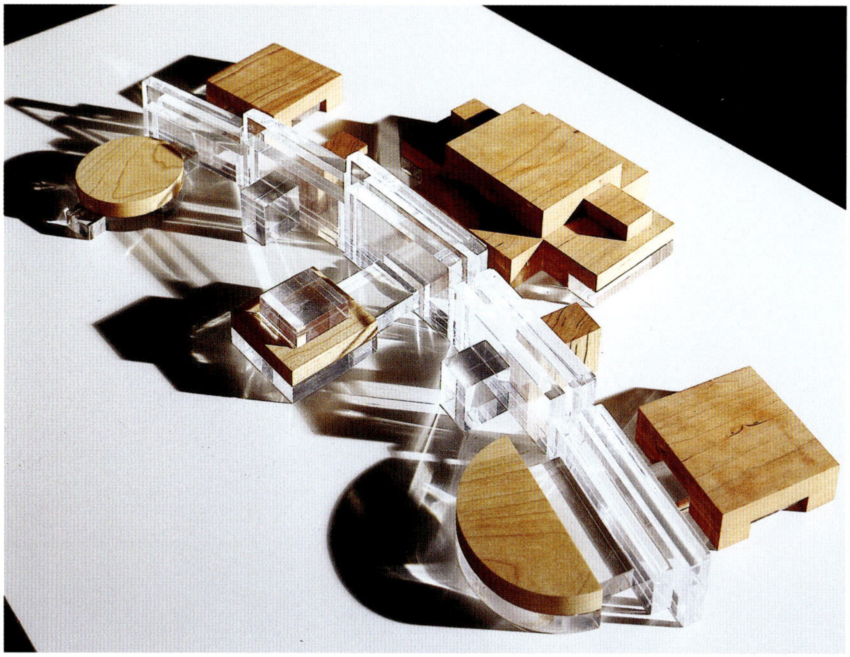

Massing study model of an unbuilt project showing a glass spine with building functions, in John's words, "being what they needed to be," extending to either side.

Hall of the Nosler House with niches and openings from main space to subspace.

Niches at the Thodos Office in Carmel.

MAIN SPACE-SUBSPACE HIERARCHY: THE NICHE AND THE EXTRUSION

Thodos loved creating a major space not as a pure cube, but with elements that attach and push out, thereby creating subspaces off the main space—always clearly articulating between the two. Forms coming together always needed to be distinct in vertical and horizontal planes, set back from one another at the corners and tops. As perhaps the Nosler House best exemplifies, for John this approach meant that a building, or even a space, would never simply have four exterior corners; the Nosler House has eighty-four.

John's design process typically began with the intention of allowing the functions to determine their own course, without a preconceived three-dimensional image in mind. To create form, he would often take the two-dimensional floor plan and extrude it upward, manipulating the heights of the differing elements to allow for the clean layering of one upon the other. An element that extended beyond another horizontally also needed to extend higher than the other.

The extruded forms coming together at the Nosler House.

The Thodos Scenic Drive House in Carmel, showing the dichotomy John enjoyed between glass as transparency and glass as form.

Entrance of the Thodos Scenic Drive House: glass as transparent form and proportion.

LIGHT AND TRANSPARENCY

John often described himself as a "heliotrope," because he needed natural light and the sun. Coming from the often sun-deprived Pacific Northwest, designing buildings that connected their occupants to natural light was always one of his prime considerations. John himself was a very open person and never particularly modest. This translated into his architecture with a great sense of openness and strong continuity between the inside and outside. Often his clients weren't quite so open and needed more privacy, which he grudgingly provided.

To bring light into buildings, glass is necessary. John's use of glass (especially with the new structural sealants) was particularly well suited to the cubic forms he loved. He found that he could create a fascinating interplay between the solid and the transparent, and between proportion and scale. He always preferred giving glass three-dimensional form, rather than utilizing it as a flat plane.

The Thodos Torres Street House, viewing the main house across an exterior space from the studio's glass Inglenook form.

Nosler House living room glass: floor-to-ceiling transparency and a connection to the landscape.

John also regarded glass as an expression of free form within a frame, where a straight plane of glass was usually notched with a prismatic play of proportion. His glass forms create dialectic Gestalt that constantly bring the viewer back and forth from perception of form to transparency and what is beyond. For the Nosler House, the garden became part of the experience of being in the house; the inside and outside would be one.

Nosler House living room glass sill: subtle movements of the glass planes express the freedom of the glass from the structure.

The independence of the human body is expressed in the freestanding doorway at the Thodos Scenic Drive House.

PROPORTION

The Greek influence also guided John's sense of proportion. He was captivated by the Golden Ratio, which is found in nature and was first formally integrated into architecture by the ancient Greeks. He tried integrating the "golden proportion" of 1:1.614 into his work whenever possible. In fact, John found the Golden Ratio so appealing that he had his drafting triangles custom-fabricated to this proportion. He simply needed to draw the diagonal when sketching to get the proportion he felt was right.

The door portal in concrete form at the Thodos Scenic Drive House.

SCALE AND THE PORTAL

Proportion also relates to "scale"—a nebulous term for many—which for John always was related to how people felt in the spaces that he created. Proportion was very intuitive for him, not just mathematical. He would often say to his assistants, "This is just out of scale!" Then adjustments would be made until it "felt" right to him. His goal was to achieve rooms that felt good to be in and buildings that fit into their contexts. Thus John's term "Modern Humanism" went beyond the use of warm, natural materials—and very much included scale and proportion.

The door portal was the ultimate symbol of how John treated Modern Humanism, and of how he represented the primacy of the individual person in his work. A Thodos-designed portal allows the individual to pass through what appears to be freestanding frame, with nothing above and nothing to the sides. First using the portal in 1979 with his own home on Scenic Drive in Carmel, John placed multiple portals throughout the Nosler House.

LAYERING

Although John was trying to create cubic, orthogonal forms, he never wanted to make them simplistic. He enjoyed multiple cubic forms coming together and intersecting. One significant technique he used was that of "layering." Designing in a two-dimensional elevation, he was always trying to achieve multiple planes rather than keeping a wall straight; in fact, his ideal was five or more planes.

The door portal in red steel at the Nosler House. This photo also shows the multiple layers and planes within a single view.

Layering from the Nosler House, here using glass block, wood, and glass.

A beautiful example of John's layering techniques from the Torres Street House in Carmel. Here you have the layers expressed in different materials—glass, steel, wood, and concrete.

DETAIL

How the materials came together, and how this was done in detail, was critical for John. He took great joy in designing these intersections to express what he needed them to say. One ubiquitous detail, also used in the Nosler House, is the way an exterior beam is expressed—extending below the siding and showing "the muscle," as John would say. And wherever possible, he loved to use custom glass detailing, which reached its apex with this project.

MATERIALITY

Much of the character of the Thodos style hinged on John's material palette. His Modern Humanism relies on the use of natural finished wood, concrete, glass, and white plaster—plus metal and steel painted bright red to make them stand out. "Ferrari red," he called it. While the Noslers allowed him to paint 625 Hobart with the colors he preferred, they also demanded—and were willing to pay for—the highest level of excellence throughout, enabling the talented construction team to achieve a quality in their craftsmanship unmatched in John's career.

What made John's architecture significant is how he synthesized these influences, interests, and inclinations into a style all his own. He worked almost obsessively on similar themes and elements of his architectural language over the course of his career, ultimately resulting in the Nosler House. The House of Light was a project that, unbeknownst to John, would be his final work. And it truly is his magnum opus.

Left: The structure is acknowledged as the beam extends below the siding of the Nosler House. This was a detail John loved and used throughout his career. He described it as "expressing the muscle" of the building.

THE DESIGN PROCESS

John Thodos working in his home studio in Carmel-by-the-Sea.

A COLLABORATION BEGINS

After determining their new 625 Hobart Street home would be Modern, and having chosen Modern architect John Thodos, the Noslers set out to provide a detailed program on which to base his design. First there was the requirement for a barrier-free house that accommodated Kay's future use of a wheelchair as well as her 90-year-old mother, Grace, who would be living with them. In addition to bedrooms for Peter and Kay, and Grace, they needed a bedroom-sized room for Kay's quilting studio, a bedroom for overnight caregivers, plus a guest room—a total of five bedrooms. Peter required a modest office and the then-standard spaces of living room, dining room, kitchen, some sort of entertainment area, and storage.

John couldn't have asked for a better project: a completely new home for clients who loved his work—and whom he respected and enjoyed working with; a presumption that the house would be designed in his Modern style; and a budget that could accommodate his passion for fine craftsmanship, quality materials, and custom detailing. From the start, all parties agreed that very few "off-the-shelf" products or materials would be used—and that John would be free to design something truly original and special.

John's enthusiasm at the time was palpable. Despite having a wonderful office in downtown Carmel, for this project he wanted to seclude himself in his home-studio, thereby minimizing distractions and enhancing his creative process. He had designed this space just for this purpose, and used it for painting and design sketching. There he would sit with his sketchbooks and tracing paper to design the House of Light.

THE SPINE

Perhaps due to the relatively long, narrow configuration of 625 Hobart Street's infill lot with a short street side, from the first sketches it was clear that the spine would form the new home's organizing principle, the "parti," for the design. As previously mentioned, the concept of the spine had obsessed John Thodos for most of his career, and now it seemed particularly well suited to this project.

John also knew that in collaboration with the Noslers and their builder, he could design the spine of his dreams. No compromises would need to be made, so the spine could provide the home's primary circulation. It would be wide, providing an ample, gracious "room" for Kay and Grace to circulate among the different parts of the home. It also would be sky-lit, making it even more street-like, thereby allowing the occupants to be in constant touch with the natural world, to experience how natural light changes throughout the day—not to mention creating a powerful dramatic space that ritualized movement through the residence.

The required elements of the program would form rooms off the spine and be linked primarily by the spine itself. The rooms could be the size and configuration the Noslers wished them to be, while allowing ample exterior space and landscape between them, and bring in natural light on three sides. John utilized his extrusion technique to project the forms in plan into three dimensions, thereby creating a hierarchy of spine to room to subspace/niche that allowed each form to be read distinctly. He realized that by working through this problem, each room could receive natural light from as many as four sides. Acting as the fourth side to bring in light, the sky-lit hall would be the tallest element of the structure. When rooms required separation, clerestory glass would separate them from the main hall.

John envisioned a "fulcrum" between a more public wing of the house towards the street, and the more private wing with the bedrooms and quilting studio. The solid forms of the building would terminate, and between the two would be located a pure-glass space containing the stair and board-form, concrete-encased elevator. The glazing would make the space feel like an outdoor room between two detached structures while bringing needed light into the lower level. In addition, the House of Light afforded John an opportunity to make rather virtuosic use of glass and minimal steel elements.

The completed scale model of the Nosler House, at the end of the schematic design phase, showing the extruded forms intersecting.

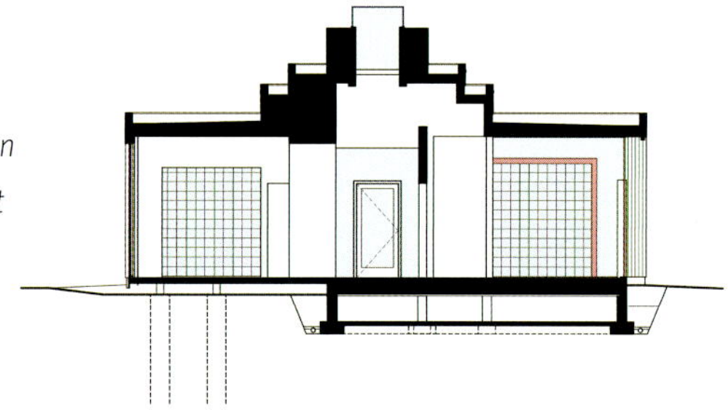

Building sections showing spatial interpenetration and how the adjacent spaces open up to the light from the spine/hall.

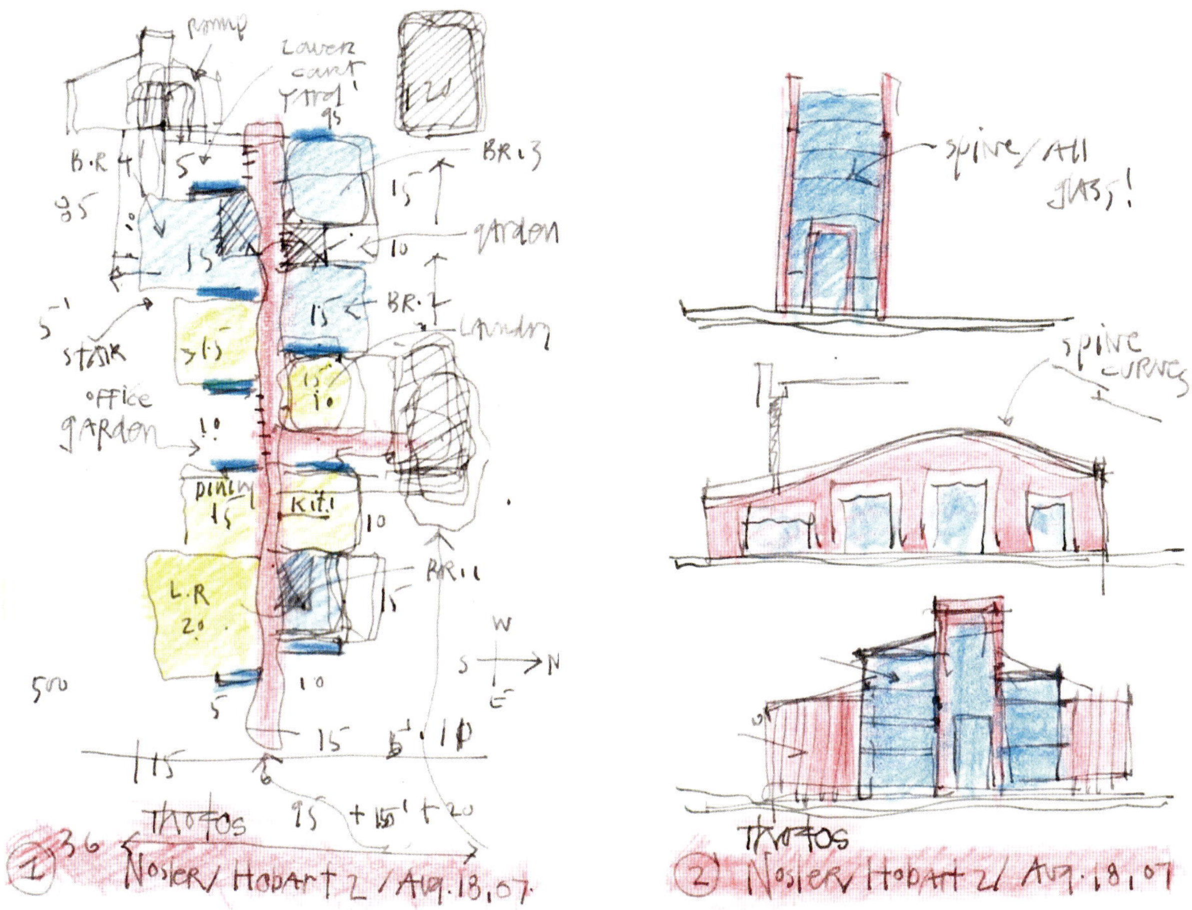

Early sketches of the Nosler House showing the hall/spine linking the spaces on either side with gardens and light in between.

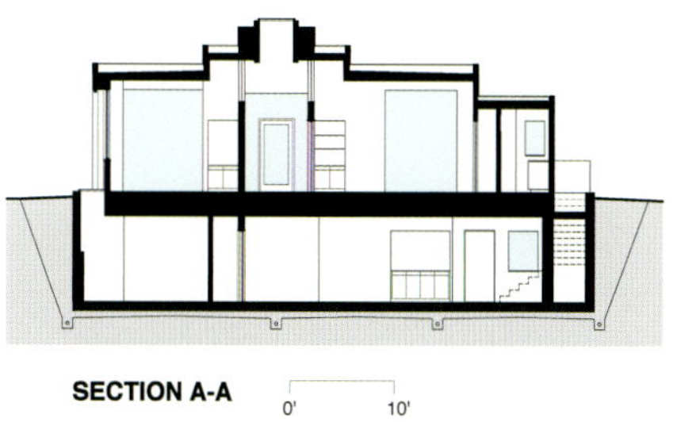

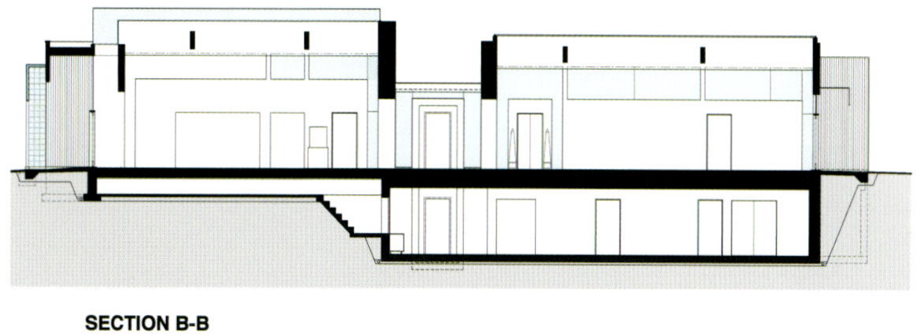

Building sections and floor plan of the Nosler House.

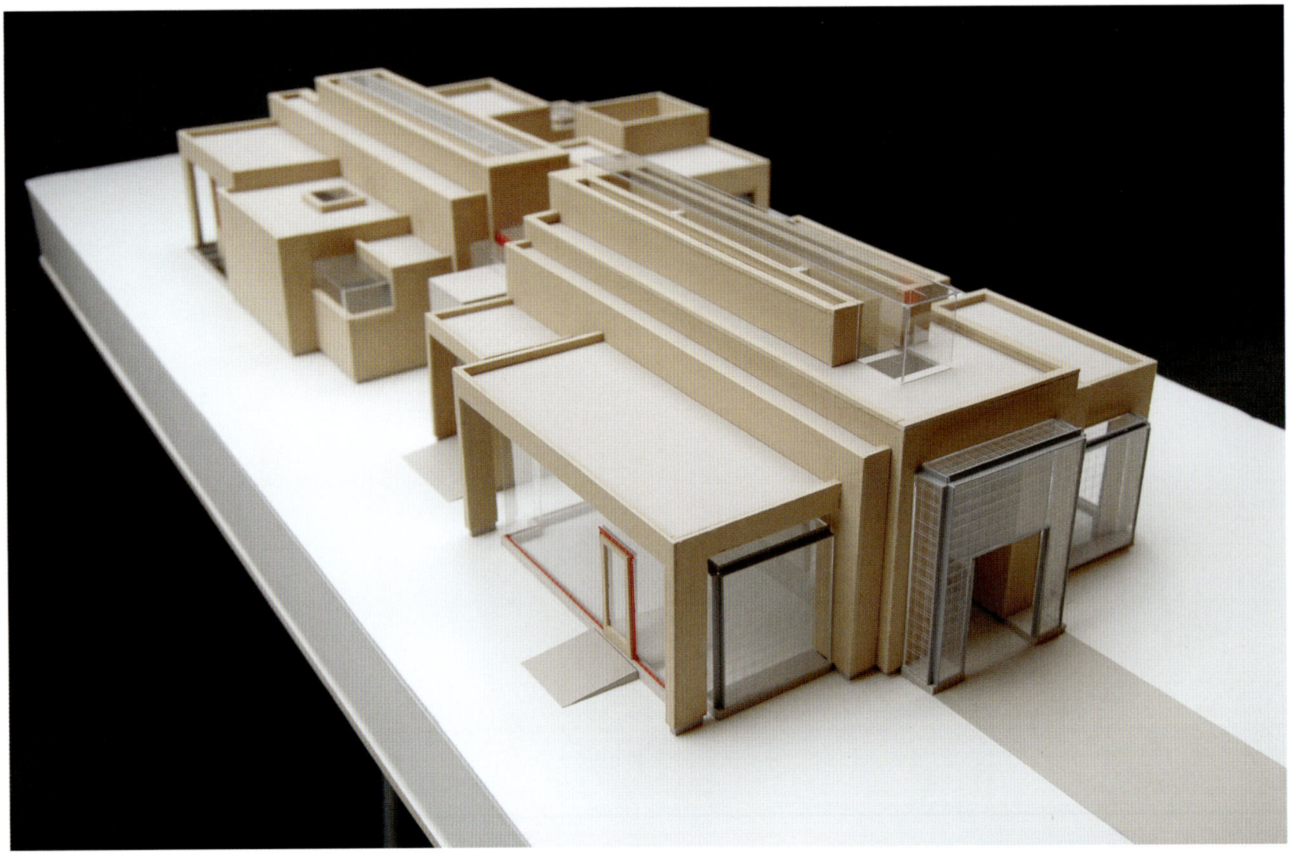

From the model, final form intersections were refined and eventually integrated into the construction drawings.

The model was used as a touchstone throughout the construction document process for understanding the original and essential design intent. As with the glass atrium, here the lightness and transparency expressed in the model needed to translate successfully into built form.

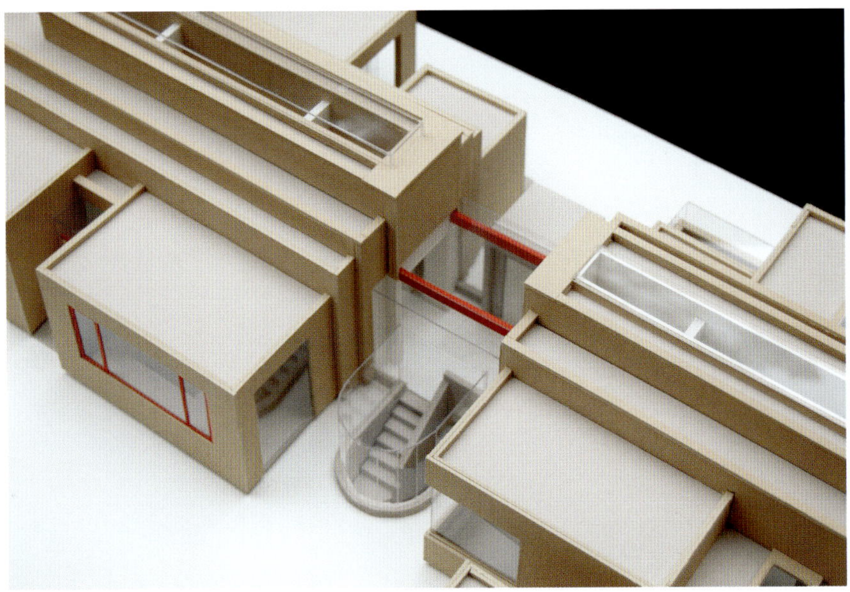

MODEL SOLUTIONS

John liked integrating the use of models into the design process. He didn't really create study models to work through different design alternatives, but after thoroughly designing in plan and elevation, he would take a fairly "final" schematic design and have a model built. Working in three dimensions, he could fine-tune the exterior form. He did all of this with the Nosler House.

The model clearly showed the form of the final building, and at 1/8" scale expressed the design's intent. It was this intent that needed to be taken through to built form; and the model served as a touchstone throughout the construction document process, to which the team referred to whenever questions arose about how a certain area should be detailed. The "feeling" conveyed by the model would have to be translated into the experience of the building. For example, the model's central atrium and spine skylight are made from plexiglass planes without support. This translated into structural sealant joints (similar to the glue used to connect the plexiglass) and as light, and minimal, a steel support structure as possible.

"MODERN" PROGRESS

Throughout the design process, John presented progress studies to Peter and Kay, who helped direct his design focus to solve functional problems about the program or discuss how a piece of art might be displayed. But regarding the home's form and general design, the Noslers gave their architect fairly free reign and encouraged him to do his best work. At the end of the schematic design phase, soon after John had presented what he thought would be the final elevation study of the four sides of the house, some disagreement arose. The street-facing elevation had been designed in a manner fairly similar to the rear elevation, with ample glass and cedar siding. It worked proportionally and was attractive.

After the Noslers went away and gave John's presentation some thought, it was Kay who spoke up. Certainly it was true that Kay had taken a longer "journey" to Modernism than Peter. But now she turned to her husband and exclaimed, "The street elevation is just not Modern enough!" At this moment, Peter had to admit that Kay was now a bona fide Modernist. It was up to him, however, to convey her feedback to their architect. John was never, shall we say, the best at accepting criticism, and was not one to hold back his frustration. With a bit of trepidation, Peter called the Thodos Studio and explained how Kay felt: the house wasn't Modern enough and needed to make a bigger statement on the street while still providing some privacy. That afternoon, Peter calmly absorbed the predictable explosion that took place on the other end of the phone call, along with its abrupt conclusion.

The following day, however, John called Peter back to say that he had stayed up until 3 a.m. and had come up with a new design of the front elevation for them to see. With a big sigh, John added, "It's much better." The result of this late-night redesign session was the use of glass block forms to screen the living and dining rooms on either side of the main entry. This would make a dramatic (and Modern) architectural statement to the street and obscure direct views into those rooms for privacy, yet still bring in an abundance of natural light. At night the forms would serve as lanterns to the building's approach. Kay approved, and the model was modified for the new front design. Plexiglass pieces where etched to express the pattern of the glass block and again clearly expressed John's design intent. Now one of the more difficult challenges would be translating this new inspiration into built form.

CONTEXT

There is an uncompromising power in how John's design addresses the street and neighborhood. Peter and Kay felt this block of Hobart Street was "home." Many of their neighbors were friends, which made the Noslers confident about constructing a new house that challenged the norms of their quiet street. But as now-evolved Modernists, they wanted to make a statement that contributed to the contemporary dialogue of their neighborhood and community: namely that Modernism and architectural excellence need not be "dumbed down" to fit in. They wanted a house that didn't take its cues from the eclectically predictable mix of houses along their street, but instead from the highest architectural ideals they had been following for years.

For his part, John Thodos always believed in relating to his context through scale, mass, and proportion—but he never let a particular context keep him from meeting his standards for his architecture. As with Carmel, he saw on Hobart Street a broad range of styles to which his architectural language could be added. John viewed the relationship between his work and the neighborhood as a positive friction; it added excitement and challenged the context to strive for excellence as the project developed. The Nosler House distinctively expresses this friction. Today the Hobart Street neighbors have found—perhaps having become familiarized with this unconventional structure over time—that the presence of a Modern home of such quality on their block is indeed a positive and exciting addition.

625 Hobart Street with the Nosler House completed.

CONSTRUCTION DETAIL

As the design process progressed, the project moved into the design development and construction document phases. More functional and aesthetic challenges needed to be addressed. The basic spaces in the floor plan were laid out and provided excellent accessibility, which also had to be integrated into the smaller scale: handrails, cabinetry, bathroom, and kitchen elements, etc. Despite their need for universal accessibility, the Noslers didn't want this functionality to be conspicuous. The challenge was to build accessibility into the home with the necessary elements appearing integral to the overall design and aesthetics of the spaces. The kitchen island was lowered and the cabinets included a subtle handrail; grab bars were installed along the showers and tubs without detracting from the quality of the spaces.

The tub room with handrails seamlessly integrated into the design of the tub surround. The cubical skylight brings in the natural world while still providing privacy.

ENGINEERING THE DESIGN

Again, the detailing of the project was always being connected back to John's original design intent. More consultants were brought in as the design developed and were directed towards this goal. No less than three structural engineering firms were used for the project. One was for the home's overall structural design. Then John engaged a Carmel engineer, with whom he liked working closely, expressly to create the most minimal structural steel supports possible for the glass atrium and spine skylight. This was easier said than done since glass structures needed to be engineered to be walked on if necessary. Peter also brought in a San Francisco firm specializing in glass design to engineer the structural sealant joints down to an eighth of an inch for accommodating possible movement during a seismic event.

The kitchen island was designed at a lower height to provide a workspace for wheelchair access plus a regular table height for an eating area. Grab bars directly below the countertop provide a location to hang towels and provide support.

As completed, the glass ceiling atrium is truly unique. Enough said.

GLASS

John developed custom glass detailing for the entire house, utilizing his signature red frames that give a crisp accent wherever the glass meets wall, ceiling, or floor. As previously discussed, the glass block was a particular challenge. John wanted "pure" glass block forms (without frames) at the front of the house. Finally he found an Italian manufacturer who could provide glass block corner pieces that eliminated the need for steel frames in this conspicuous location. Minimal steel T-bars were utilized to support the horizontal glass block at the top. Another challenge was the living room, whose design lacked sufficient lateral support. Because an additional large steel frame would have destroyed the design intent, the solution became a narrow steel rod that could extend down to provide the needed support.

The corner glass block.

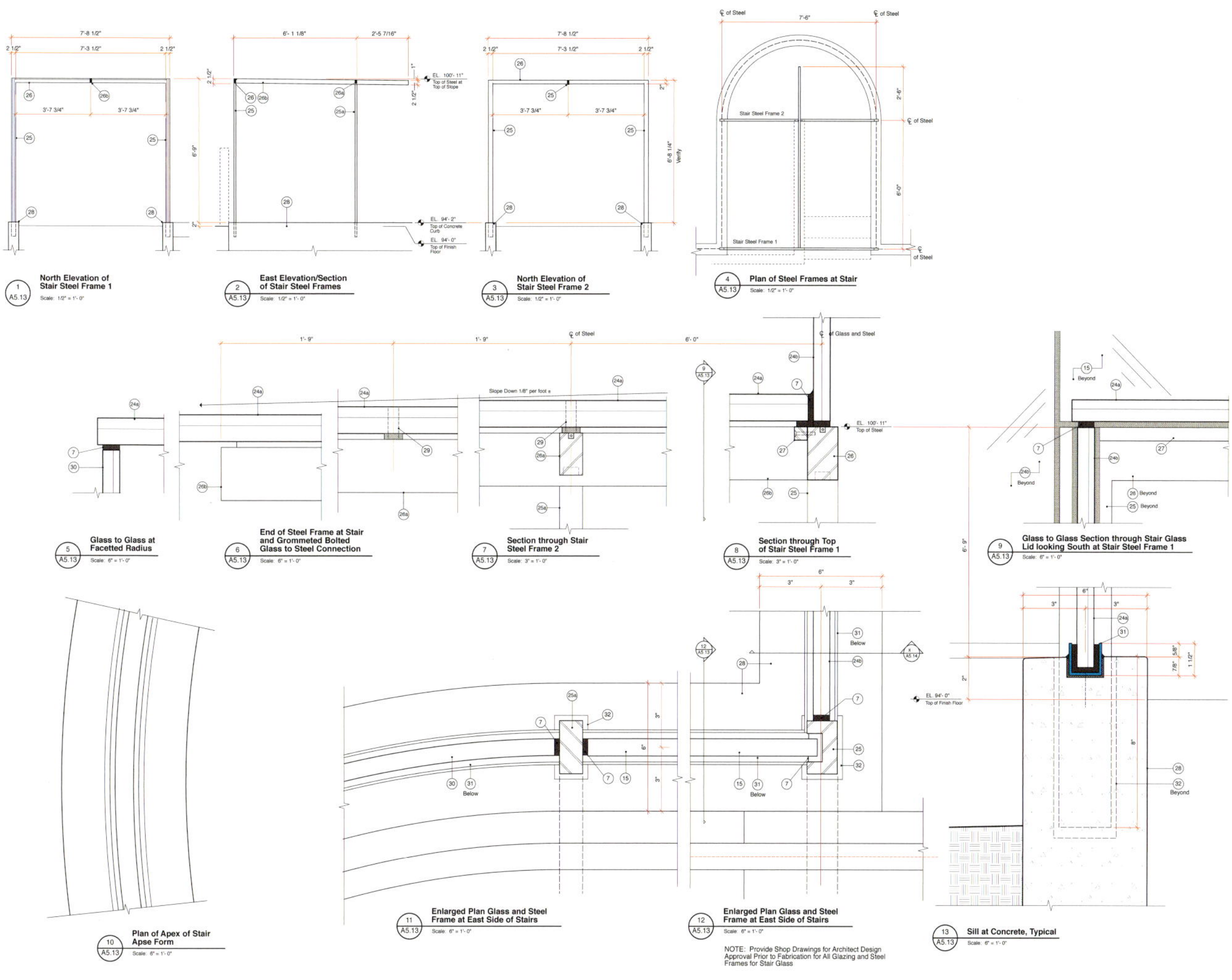

Construction details for the atrium glass.

PORTALS

John's signature door portals required special attention when it came to detailing. These overt symbols of the human scale of the individual mandated that glass freely extend at the sides and above. Typically doorframes extend from floor to ceiling, providing structural support at bottom and top. In the Nosler House, the steel frame would need to act as a vertical cantilever, providing enough bracing at the bottom to let it stand freely in glass. Refer to the door in the living room photograph on page 144.

PROTECTING THE REDWOOD

The dining room presented another structural challenge. Directly outside was a large, gorgeous redwood tree with an extensive root system. By necessity, the corner of the dining room needed to come fairly close to the tree. The team devised a structural system that used steel beams to cantilever out, and then—with narrow, stainless steel rods—suspend the floor out near the corner. John loved the idea of these two small rods piercing through the interior space to subtly acknowledge the structural gymnastics that were actually going on. The result was that this magnificent tree became part of the space—acting as the "added diner" at the table, Peter says.

The dining room showing the steel rod that suspends the floor structure to protect the roots of the adjacent redwood tree.

WOOD

John Thodos loved wood and fine wood craftsmanship for his interior spaces. For the House of Light, though, he wanted extensive white plaster walls to provide the screen on which natural light played throughout the day. So he introduced rift-sawn white oak for the floors baseboards and door trims to bring warmth to the interior. Knowing he could rely on the craftsmanship of the builders, he designed a low white oak baseboard that would be flush with the plaster walls—not an easy detail to construct. John also utilized minimal white oak door trims that projected slightly from the plaster, acting as portals from one space to another. Neither of these subtle details was standard; therefore they gave the Nosler House a sense of uniqueness and craftsmanship that would set life within its walls apart from anywhere else.

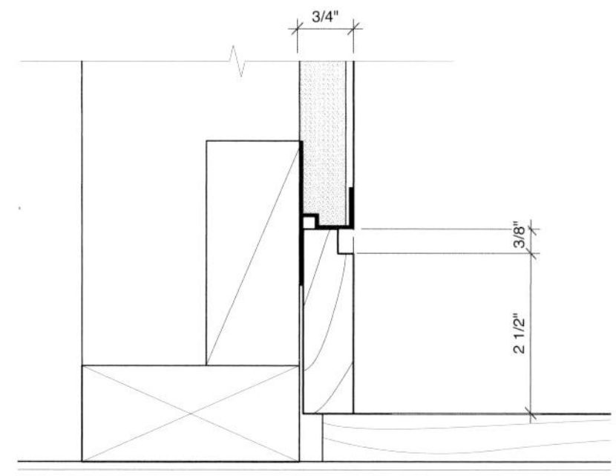

Interior white oak flush baseboard detail.

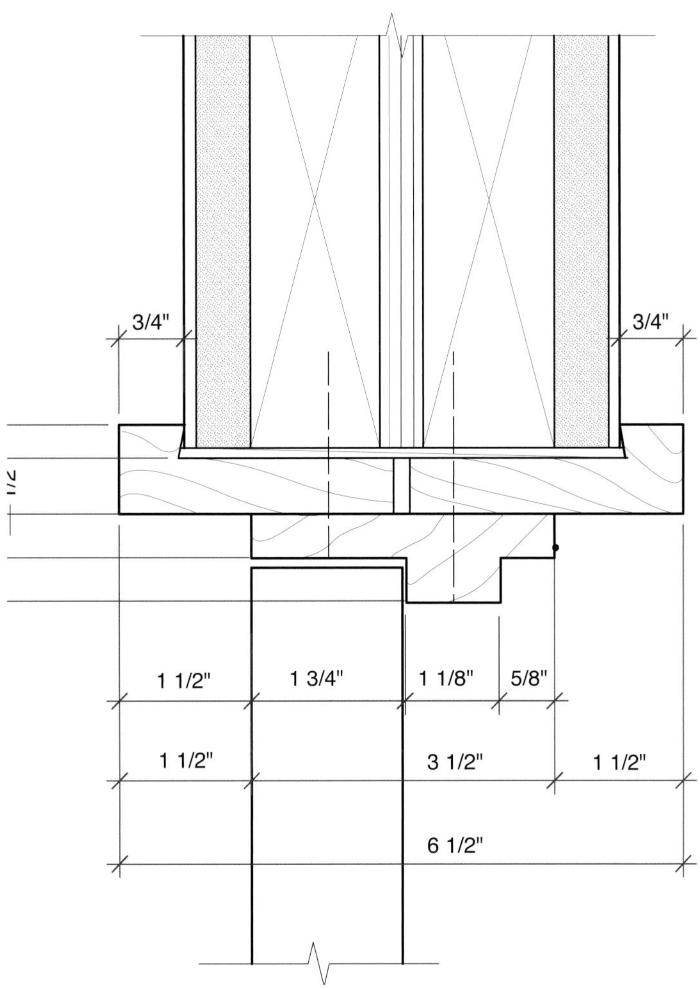

Another of John's subtle ideas is the elegant interior doorframe. Again it is rarely noticed yet has such an impact. The usual piece of trim that covers the open joint between the doorframe and the wall is gone. The doorframe itself provides the needed closure.

THE NEXT CHALLENGE

By the end of the design and construction document process, it was clear that John would be challenging the builders on all fronts. Nothing about 625 Hobart Street was simple or would not require the highest degree of skill and craftsmanship to achieve. John had designed a home that was a culmination of his architectural development. To bring the House of Light to life would not be a fast process nor inexpensive. Yet for their part, Peter and Kay only pushed John to do his best work.

There was an auspicious occurrence during the middle of the design process that greatly helped this pursuit of excellence along. A few years earlier, Peter had become a primary investor in a startup company established by his son, Zander—who had invented a coffee maker that made what many felt was the perfect single-cup of coffee. It was such a successful product that Zander sold his company to another coffee company by the name of Starbucks. The timing couldn't have been better. Peter, as one of the main investors, reaped a handsome dividend and was able to direct some of the profits into the new house at 625 Hobart Street.

Now the Noslers' high expectations, and perhaps John's most accomplished design of his career, would be matched with a construction budget that accommodated the uncompromised realization of their dreams. The responsibility for bringing all of this to fruition would fall to Greg Marrone, of Marrone & Marrone Construction. We follow that story next.

GALLERY

CONSTRUCTION

Greg Marrone, whom Peter chose as the general contractor for the Nosler House, was accustomed to the world of high-end residential construction. Greg describes it as "a perfect storm of architects who want to stretch their creative side; clients who (while often decisive and focused in their business world) can tend toward indecisiveness and tardiness when working on such a personal project; and interior designers who often miss the architect's intent and/or the hidden budget, and do not have backgrounds in a more solid business setting."

THE SCENARIO

Greg believed these circumstances often resulted in team members with competing interests but no clear leader. The homeowners, who by default of paying the bills are the final decision makers, rarely have the time and expertise necessary to lead the team effectively. And he believed another frequent design challenge revolved around the landscape designer, who typically enters the process very late, being frustratingly doomed to live with issues that can't be changed. Fortunately, Greg didn't face such a scenario with the Nosler House. He had a team leader in Peter Nosler, with his vast knowledge of construction and organizing construction projects—and an architect in John Thodos, who was committed to working with both owner and builder to achieve the best possible results.

SYNCHRONICITY AND PERSONALITIES

Marrone & Marrone was an auspicious, even stellar, choice to build the House of Light. But as often is the case, it was personalities and synchronicity that brought this team together. Peter and Kay Nosler had enjoyed working with interior designer Elizabeth Hill on their two previous homes, and wanted her involved with the new house. Peter well knew how very protective John Thodos was when it came to controlling the design of his projects, and that he tended to regard interior designers more as a threat to his vision rather than as professionals who could enhance it. This came from difficult past experiences, and perhaps is where the term "interior desecrator" resides in the vocabularies of many architects. Peter knew from the start that John would likely have an adversarial relationship with Elizabeth, who was forewarned. She took Peter's communication of the architect's sensitivities to heart.

So while Elizabeth was somewhat kept in the background, she did make a most important contribution. When Peter asked Elizabeth—who was a very popular local designer and knew many of the best builders in the vicinity—which construction firms she would recommend, she thought not of a general contractor but rather of a project superintendent with whom she had worked several times: Steve Gonzalez—a nice, mild-mannered gentleman who had run the most efficient, quality-driven job sites with which she had been associated. Alongside Steve's excellence as a builder, she recalled his tendency to want everyone to be happy. Elizabeth thought he would work well with the not-so-mild-mannered, passionate John Thodos.

MARRONE IS HIRED

It so happened that Steve had just begun working for a general contractor named Greg Marrone, and a meeting was soon arranged between Peter and Greg. It went well. Although Greg was a graduate of UC Berkeley, he came from a background of furniture and cabinet making before moving into general contracting. This sensibility, plus his attention to detail and craft, would be a perfect match for a most demanding owner and his equally demanding architect.

MEETING THE ARCHITECT

Now it was time to meet John Thodos. At this point, the design was solidly in the design development phase and moving into construction documents. The construction team would be led by Greg Marrone, with Steve Gonzalez as onsite superintendent. Greg and Steve drove down to Carmel to meet with John at his home studio, where he had been ensconced for a while, working exclusively on the Nosler residence. In addition to the drawings and the model, the studio (and the adjacent main home) provided the builders with a sense of material and detail that were hallmarks of the Thodos style—with which they would be entrusted to bring to the new Nosler home at Menlo Park's 625 Hobart Street.

As Steve recalls, they had timed the 90-minute drive in order to be exactingly punctual. They had even dressed up somewhat, realizing this was not just a day on the job site, and wanting to make a good first impression on the formidable John Thodos. They waited patiently after Judy Thodos had seated them. John didn't arrive at the studio on time, despite living next door. It should be said that working virtually from home had made the workday more efficient and productive for him, but meant that some of the formalities of dressing up and going to the office were relaxed. Eventually John meandered over from the house, introduced himself to the construction team, and seated himself behind his desk. Although for members of the Thodos team such behavior wasn't that unusual, it did make an impression on the Marrone team: John was dressed solely in his signature bathrobe.

While waiting for John to greet them, Steve construed that John regarded himself as a "one-of-a-kind" architect who would be determined to call the shots from the start. It was not unusual for John to behave in this manner as he instinctively sought to establish dominance over others on the project team from the beginning. He wanted the message to be clear: Thodos was in charge and not someone to be trifled with in any manner. With that said, John's appreciation, admiration, and respect for builders who met his expectations were very strong—and he quickly developed such confidence in the Marrone team.

Acting as the proverbial single-car garage for the property, John Thodos was at his contemporary best here, with both a north-facing window and an all-glass "Inglenook" (subspace off the main space) with a fireplace in his inspiring office-studio.

GLASS AND GLAZING

As construction drawings were being developed, Greg's primary concern was the extensive use of glass. The architectural glass detailing was extensive, but a glass subcontractor had to be chosen, shop drawings prepared, and the glazing would have to meet stringent energy code and seismic requirements. Greg took on the responsibility of getting the glazing submittal ready for implementation. Peter hired a specialized structural engineer expressly to review the final detailing and sizing of every structural sealant joint to accommodate potential seismic movement. In the end, the envisioned glasswork was so new and unusual that the subcontractor had to revise his pricing two or three times.

Clearly the pricing of the glass was the project's toughest challenge. Rather than a fixed price, which the Noslers ultimately would receive after two attempts, the total cost was still in unknown territory due to the very unique design. Ultimately a compromise was reached after the job was completed, with both the Noslers and the glass contractor less than satisfied but much the wiser. But the time and meticulous thought that went into the House of Light's glazing paid off, as the completed work would meet everyone's expectations and requirements. Indeed the final product expressed the full design intent shown in that original 1/8" scale architectural model.

CONSTRUCTION BEGINS

Construction began on the Nosler House in August 2008. With the large lower basement level to be constructed first, it was doubtful that extensive work above ground could commence before the rainy season began; this could slow the project considerably. Peter brought his commercial experience to bear: although highly unusual for a single-family residential project, he ordered roof trusses that would span across the site so the entire footprint of the building could be tented, thereby allowing work to progress on schedule throughout the rainy season. This unorthodox but creative solution saved a huge amount of time. Neighbors had to wonder whether some extraordinary ancient artifacts, or perhaps dinosaur bones, were being collected from this major archaeological dig occurring on their street.

When the City of Menlo Park's permit-review process delayed the groundbreaking from the spring to October, Peter designed this temporary rain-shedding roof to allow the lower-level work to proceed.

A simple, concrete-walled lower level could have just four corners, but not here. The reality of 84 corners on the upper level exterior had its beginnings here on the lower level.

Spring arrived and the upper level was well underway, with the formwork of the lower level's complex curved stairway almost complete.

The curved glass wall at the stairway to the lower level was being braced, awaiting installation of the glass ceiling over the stairs. Facing north, it draws warm and inviting natural light.

Top quality was expected of all elements of the construction. The concrete was no exception, and it was the first—but pretty much the only—casualty of these exacting requirements. The concrete of the stairway's apse form was to be exposed, with meticulous forms created that used the same cedar siding for the exterior's main cladding. This in turn created a wonderful, light-wood grain on the grey concrete and clear vertical lines of the boards extending around the curve. Let's be clear, though: building with concrete, especially this type of board-form material, is expensive and time-consuming. Unfortunately, when the stair wall was initially poured, the quality fell short and owner, builder, and architect rejected the work. A concrete wall with extensive steel reinforcement throughout is not easy to remove and demolish, yet this was done.

A new concrete subcontractor was hired and a new wall was poured, this time meeting the team's standards and expectations. Greg described the experience as a wake-up call that made him insist on only the best subcontractors and craftsmen to complete the rest of the project. Steve also took the situation to heart, realizing how special the Nosler House was. He strove to get every subcontractor and workman on the team to "invest emotionally in the project and make it their own."

Both Steve and Greg had worked on Contemporary, Modern homes where tolerances were notoriously minimal. Other architectural styles make extensive use of trim that simply covers up any joint that isn't exacting. In much of the detailing in Modern architecture, everything is exposed. However, the Nosler House brought this precision detailing to another level, for which the construction team was fully prepared. Steve knew that in order to make the finished product look right, the hidden substrate (e.g., framing) for all finishes must be constructed as perfectly as the exposed materials. For example, in order to accentuate the continuity of inside to outside, John required that the exterior finish of the cedar siding be exactly flush and aligned with the interior's thin-coat plaster sheetrock.

Another exacting requirement was that the face of the white oak baseboards must align and flush out with the plaster finish of the sheetrock walls. Installation of the vertical cedar siding was more akin to cabinetwork than the usual use of wood siding. Corners of the siding had to be perfectly aligned and each glued together. As previously noted, a simpler structure would have perhaps four corners; the Nosler House has some 84 of them. This involved an amount of time and attention to detail for which many clients have neither the patience nor the funds. To Peter Nosler's great credit, he provided the team with sufficient time and budget to work through the complexities, allowing everything to turn out according to plan.

The glazed awning over the back door is yet another detail well designed and executed. The crisp red steel frame allows the glass to cleanly terminate into the cedar siding.

Seen here in the dining room, John Thodos made his farewell visit to what would be his final and, perhaps, greatest, project. Sadly, this occurred just weeks before his death.

ARCHITECT'S FAREWELL

Steve remembers that in late summer 2009, John visited the construction site for what would be the last time. A working relationship that began abrasively had evolved into one of mutual respect and, perhaps, some affection. The framing had been completed and the spaces were defined. No longer could John stand for extended periods of time, so Steve found him a chair, which they first placed in the spine/hallway. John sat there for five or ten minutes, repeating this process for each room in the house, which allowed him to experience each space and envision how it would be when completed. At this point, he probably knew he was dying and was savoring one of the great joys of an architect: experiencing the achievement of a creative vision now manifesting in the world as the result of a painstaking design process. How fitting that John concluded his career with the Nosler House: the culmination of his design explorations, and the perfecting of an architectural language all his own.

John's last trip to the Nosler House was such a touching moment. Standing inside the house-in-progress, he clearly was very proud of what he and his great team had achieved. He was especially happy to make this special gift possible to Kay Nosler, whom he so admired.

John stands at the end of the framed spine/hall in the back of the house, envisioning the completed home he wouldn't live to see.

As John arose from the chair in the last room, he walked over to Steve and Don, the construction manager, each of whom received a big, long hug from this emotional and sincere Greek-American. His final words were, "I love the bones!" I think that his embrace of these two men was a thank-you for doing justice to his design, as well as a final—and classically "Thodos"—directive to finish it right. John passed away on November 16, 2009, comforted and gratified knowing that his last and greatest work was in the hands of Marrone & Marrone and his greatest client, Peter Nosler. He was right to trust them. Thanks to their efforts, the House of Light was completed several months later—a reflection of, and a tribute to, John's formidable architectural vision.

THE GARDEN

John Thodos designed the Nosler House as the apotheosis of his architectural style, based on the requirements and lifestyle of Peter and Kay Nosler. When landscape architect William Peters came into the process, the design was already complete and construction had begun. John envisioned a house set in a garden. With his extensive use of glass, he knew the connection of inside to outside was an essential part of this architecture. But his design process was independent of anything specific beyond the confines of the building itself.

Beyond the walls of wood and glass, William Peters was left to design and create the landscape in which this Thodos building sits, without much input from John, although he certainly provided the exceptional architecture. William's process took this as the starting point for generating and inspiring his design for the House of Light's garden. He saw in the home's strong architectural forms, and in the many walls of full-height glass, the means to connect interior and exterior spaces.

But William also recognized 625 Hobart Street as a home with clearly defined rooms, unlike much Modern architecture with its open plans lacking definition. After all, the Nosler House was conceived as a series of rooms, enveloped by clear forms, connected by a spine. Therefore, William viewed his task as finding the correct dialogue of each room with its outside counterpart. "Each room had its own personality and character," he says. "It was all about making a sympathetic and inspiring connection for each." Thus William started the specific design work once the house was actually framed, when he could see the forms and scale and feel the spaces. He visualized and imagined the garden by putting himself into each of the rooms.

The narrow south side yard and walkway with the door portal to the small office and living room beyond.

LIVING ROOM GARDEN

William began here. This room faces the street and the narrow side yard. The glass block obscures the view to the street, so the room opens up to the side yard. There are just planes of glass from floor to ceiling, which allow the interior and exterior space to be experienced as one.

At the fence, William provided a tall hedge for a border and for privacy. In front of the hedge, he located a low stone wall and foot path. Built by artisan masons, the stone wall is a crafted work of art. It functions on the outside to provide (1) a layered border at the property edge and (2) an architectural element for the path's edge that leads down the length of the house. For the living room, it serves as one side of the room.

The south walkway looking west, running from living room to back garden. The tall hedge helps provide privacy and a border to the extended living room space. The low stone wall artfully provides an intermediate scale to the hedge.

The living room and south walkway. Note how the hedge and low stone wall, along with the exterior wood siding of the wall enclosing Peter's office, act as borders to the space because of the floor-to-ceiling glass.

Tall redwoods, like this one by the dining room, suit the home's tall structure. Japanese maples and lower plant materials help pull down the scale of the garden.

DINING ROOM GARDEN

This room is unique because of the large redwood tree in such proximity to the window. The structural design to allow for this proximity and maintain the tree's health has previously been discussed, but the tree's size can feel a bit overwhelming for the room. William felt the space needed a way to "cozy-up" to the tree. So he used small-scale woodland plants at the base of the tree to provide a foreground to this view and create an intermediate scale. On the east side facing the street, a Japanese maple is planted directly outside the glass block, allowing for a dance of the leaves through light, shadow, and form through the translucent material.

Right: Structural accommodations preserved this huge California redwood by the driveway, by the dining room glass wall.

KITCHEN GARDEN

The kitchen had two different conditions. Along the north side, there's a narrow space between the driveway and the window at the counter and sink. William uses a row of Japanese maples. They're pruned to provide nice light and views, but are so close to the window that you get the sense you're in a tree house when preparing food or washing dishes.

The western window faces the glass stairwell. One of the wonderful elements John often used in his work was creating visual links from one part of a building to another across open landscape. Being able to look across a garden from one interior space to see someone in another part of the house creates a unique connection. William planted things that were small and detailed with seasonal color and interest. Milkweed plants attract butterflies, and sitting for lunch at mid-day looking through the window is enchanting.

Japanese maples temper the light pouring into the kitchen, north over the driveway. Sitting at table height vs. bar height varies the view of the garden.

Being among the trees at the kitchen sink.

The apse form of the stairway pushing out into the garden.

The garden encroaching on, and merging with, the glass atrium space.

ATRIUM GARDEN

In the glass atrium, with the complete transparency of the space and lushness of the landscape, one feels—in an even more intense way—the experience of being inside, yet also, a part of the garden itself.

QUILTING STUDIO GARDEN

The master bedroom and Kay's quilting studio face the backyard, which has ample space to create a larger garden experience. By the time William began designing it, Kay's illness had progressed to the point where she could no longer easily access the garden. But the tall, glass cube/volume designed by John allowed her to almost be there from her studio.

The bay window of Kay's quilting studio extending into the garden with Japanese maples and roses.

The transparent volume extends into the landscape surrounded and framed by Japanese maples. Beyond is a low hedge that forms the rose garden. Kay loved roses and personally chose the varietals. William writes:

"These are tree roses, which produce volumes of brightly colored flowers that appear to be perched on the top of the hedge. The hedge acts as the foreground but also serves to anchor these delicate flowers in this otherwise natural garden."

Right: The floor-to-ceiling glass of the master bedroom as seen from the garden.

MASTER BEDROOM GARDEN

On the opposite side of the spine hall is the master bedroom. It has a window framed above the bed facing the side yard, then opens up to floor-to-ceiling glass facing the rear garden. William created a garden "room" about the same size as the master bedroom it adjoins, visually doubling the amount of space. He envisioned the varied experiences of this sleeping room to be inextricably tied to the experience of the garden. He writes:

The extensive glass used in the master bedroom creates a sense of delight, sitting on the edge of the bed looking out at the low grasses, Japanese maple, and majestic redwoods.

"In the mornings, though, or with afternoon naps, it's the place of awakening. So, the garden wanted to be dreamy and tranquil. ...I can imagine the drowsy morning view, looking out into the maples and the woodland meadow. It's the sort of place I might like to linger, in bed, dozing, or perhaps daydreaming with my eyes closed lightly. The garden truly does have a sense of immediacy and delight."

SPINE HALL AND ENTRY

Finally, the spine hall as a room is a powerful linear form that cannot be ignored by the landscape. It moves from front yard to back yard, each side having very different characters. One of the critical decisions that had a major impact on the architecture was the approach from the street. It was William who thought of creating a diagonal path from the street to the front door of the house—which John Thodos immediately embraced as the perfect solution. After all, it was the ancient Greeks who created the notion of a promenade architecturale, an intentional processional approach to a building or sacred site. This always was done on the diagonal and obliquely and never, as the Romans did, straight on. This allowed the House of Light to be seen as three-dimensional sculptural form. What could be more appropriate for a Greek-American architect?

Right: The diagonal approach to the front entrance, where a glass block-enclosed vestibule welcomes you into the spacious hallway seen through the entry glass.

The backyard garden and small fountain front the curved, sloping Goldworthy-inspired stone wall, with one end sinking into the ground out of sight.

REAR PATIO

Looking down the spine towards the portal door at the rear, there's a path out to a small, circular patio. What ends this powerful axis is another beautiful stone wall built by the artisan masons. Here a truncated wall emerges like an ancient ruin from the ground, extending up on the diagonal to terminate the spine as the diagonal path in the front began it. Peter, inspired by the work of one of his favorite artists, Andy Goldsworthy, had suggested this to William and the masons. The result has a delightful effect. In front of the wall stands a large ceramic vase fountain with the tranquil sound of percolating water.

Red-painted epoxy and expressive metal benches provide a delightful place to sit in this tranquil garden space, while echoing the red of the home's metal-framed windows and linking the garden to the architecture. It was William's vision to create what he calls a "house in a woodland setting in the midst of a cloud of Japanese maples." Something magical happened, however, when this vision merged with the form and spaces of the architecture: garden and architecture became one.

Right: The back door duplicates the front door. This transparency allows the spine axis to terminate in an inviting outdoor room with stone wall and fountain.

LIFE IN THE HOUSE OF LIGHT

What is it like living in a House of Light?

What is it like living in a work of art?

And what is it like living in a house where everything is designed so intentionally, so uniquely, so completely for you?

These are especially interesting questions, since most people aren't fortunate to have such an opportunity. No one knew the answers better—especially in how they relate to his own work—than John Thodos, who had designed, built, and lived in two houses also created with his uncompromising vision.

By the time John left the scene, he knew that the Noslers would have this very same opportunity. On his final trip to the site, he saw the way the construction was coming together: the spaces were right, the proportions felt right, and the groundwork had been laid.

Perhaps most importantly, John had put the right people (design team, builders, and especially clients) in place to ensure the uncompromised realization of his design. Some might question the use of the word "opportunity," since Peter had paid significant amounts of money not just for "an opportunity" to live in something of this quality, but to guarantee its achievement.

Fortunately or unfortunately, this isn't how the creative process works. Great designs and architecture come together as a synergetic synthesis, where every aspect must be right. During John's last visit, he was seasoned enough to know that things were working as they should. The bones were in place for magic to happen: when light, time, and experience meet perfectly realized space and form.

To achieve greatness, a piece of architecture—and, in fact, all art—must work on many different levels simultaneously. Peter has described how each room of this house feels "so comfortable": the quality of light, the connection to the outside and garden, the openness, and how the rooms maintain a unique relationship to one another through the gracious hall that links them. But in every space you find yourself, there's something else at work. Sitting in any one spot, you become aware of multitudinous design elements forming your experience in that moment. It's not just the one thing; it's many.

EXPERIENCING THE HOUSE

As you enter through the front door, you immediately notice the different layering of light qualities—not just some light entering from one window.

There's the light from the sky above, which moves across the planes of walls as time progresses through the day. Is this house really open to the sky?

There are the lightest of steel frames periodically supporting what must be an enclosure.

There's also a bold brightness halfway down the length of the hall (from the glass atrium), which might appear slightly mysterious to a first-time visitor.

Then there's an unseen source of light coming in from the sides of the hall to be discovered.

Looking down, the red silhouette of a door beckons you to the promise of a green garden beyond.

The main hall itself is defined by walls. Most walls typically don't extend to the ceiling. There are openings as your eye moves down the passage, but they're at differing heights, with intriguing proportions, offering distinct spaces to enter or perceive. And looking downward, you might notice the finely crafted white oak baseboard. It feels just the right scale, and harmonizes so nicely with the plaster wall.

You might be sitting in the kitchen enjoying a meal, appreciating how the island is at the proper seating height, and not just a typical kitchen counter. Then someone emerges from the glass enclosed staircase—which you can only see because one can look out of the house and look into it again across a piece of the garden.

Walking down the hall into the atrium, you may feel a remarkable sensation of being outside and inside at the same time. Then you notice the form of your enclosure, yet there's only the suggestion of it, because the form is transparent—there, but not there.

Perhaps you glance at the wood against the concrete of the elevator, noticing the grain from the formwork on the concrete; yes, it matches the width of the siding boards.

Descending to the lower level, notice how the craft of the floor, baseboards, and doorframes follows you. Art and light await you at the bottom of the stairs.

You can appreciate how the light, brought in from above, plays on the white walls in the hallway and bedrooms.

Right: Moving back up the stairway, you observe the smooth, perfectly scaled stainless steel handrail, the finely crafted board-formed concrete, and the warm white oak perfectly scribed against the concrete. Looking up, there are the sky, the trees, and somehow the most thin, delicate steel imaginable.

Upstairs once again, you might be sitting in the living room and see how the light dances through the glass block. You're intrigued by the interplay between the transparency of the adjacent glass and the translucent opacity of the glass block, which is enjoyable in and of itself. You understand that, "No, I don't want to be seen from the street, but, yes, I want to be part of this garden." Happily, the choice of materials works on both functional and aesthetic levels.

Stepping back, you note the independence of the red steel frames; one framing a passage for one human figure, the other for a grid of glass block that's not only in a flat plane but extruded out, taking on a third dimension. For something to be art, sometimes it only takes the right "framing." On the opposite wall, you can delight in more art, with a painting called *Head* by Jerry McLaughlin.

Turning around you notice the undulation of the glass planes, and then the sharp "Ferrari" red of the window frame, the craft of the stone wall, and the beautiful cedar siding whose floor-to-ceiling glass helps define the room. Observe how those same glass walls intensify the floating feeling of the *Three Hanging Figures* by Francis Semple.

Moving your gaze again, you perceive a totally different quality of light entering from the spine hall. From here you notice the adjacent relationship of the three hanging sculptures, the unseen source of light, and farther across the hall, the magical painting *Four Clusters* by Robert Goodnough—which seems made for this spot.

ART AND THE ART OF LIVING

Peter and Kay's journey to falling in love with and to collecting Modern-Contemporary art, dovetailed with their falling in love with Modern-Contemporary architecture. This culminated in the impressive, and highly involving, display of art throughout their newly completed home.

Ironically, Peter doesn't recall discussing with John Thodos during the design and construction process what role the art would play in their house—despite the fact that John himself was a painter. Instead their conversations focused on light, space, and function. Nevertheless, the Nosler's finished house is a marvelous gallery. Living with their collection had become a vital part of their everyday lives; and Peter and Kay found brilliant ways to integrate carefully chosen work into the various spaces. The art both came to supplement and enhance the architecture. Their serendipitous interplay is instrumental to the powerful experience of living in this extraordinary home.

In this House of Light, there's always something more to discover and enjoy: namely the continual reflection of design-intention back into experience—not to mention the wonderfully unintentional juxtapositions that become appreciated only with living in the home. What could be more embracing and empowering than being in an environment pulsing with constant awareness of human creativity and craft—the evident care and love that went into every corner, and the knowledge that all of it was done for you?

Such is the intangible enchantment of the Nosler House.

AFTERWORD

John Thodos passed away in November 2009 without seeing the completion of his final work. Kay was able to spend her remaining time in the comfort of the environment John had created for her. More and more confined to home in her last year, having such a house allowed Kay to maintain a richness to her life not otherwise possible. Whether it was moving through the light-filled spine hall or glass atrium, sitting among her quilt creations in her studio's pure-glass, cubic bay window connected to the garden she loved, or being with friends and family in the kitchen—so often the social center of any home—John's vision made life in this home pleasant and fulfilling for Kay.

It was not just living in the completed house, but also her active involvement in the design and construction process, that brought Kay joy and meaning. In no small measure, the person responsible for the enjoyment of this process—and a critical part of the successful end result—was Steve Gonzales, the full-time superintendent who managed the 20-month building project. In addition to the daily challenges of making sure every detail was properly executed, Steve constantly engaged with Kay on how everything was going. This collaboration was exactly what she and Peter wanted, and they were able to experience it to the fullest, with Kay finding a focus beyond her illness. Another critical factor was their good fortune to live just across the street while their new home was being built.

In April 2010, the Noslers held a wonderful party in the nearly completed house and moved in over the July 4th holiday. Kay's illness took her life four months later. This is a truly sad story, but their happiness in creating the

House of Light clearly was a blessing for both of them. After Kay's passing, Peter remained in the house for many years and enjoyed the fruits of their labor-of-love endeavor. Life has continued for him. He spends time with his son Zander and his family, is very active in various philanthropic projects, and continues to travel and enjoy art and architecture around the world.

Peter's relationship with a close family friend, Julie Veitch, blossomed into love, and they propitiously married on 12/12/12. The couple now can brag that they actually own three Thodos houses, because Julie lives in Carmel and built a Thodos-designed home there in 2009! Eventually they found themselves spending most of their time in Carmel without being able to enjoy the Menlo Park property as much as they would have liked. Although Peter loved his House of Light, he realized the moment had come to pass it on and let another family experience the magic of living in this significant piece of architecture.

For Peter, this book is also a key part of the home's legacy. "Creating the house was such a complex and amazing experience that I just couldn't allow it to fade as life moved on," he notes. "Our wonderful book captures exactly what 'the right thing to do' meant to my family."

ACKNOWLEDGMENTS

For both the creation of the House of Light, as well as this book—a document that preserves this remarkable story—there are a wide range of individuals who well deserve huge thanks for making it all happen.

John Thodos has a large body of significant work that accounts for his stature in the architectural community. However, his inspiration and dedication to his design values were unparalleled on this project. His associate Erik Dyar also played a key role in the design and was able to do so much in the production of this book. Thodos Architects received a much-deserved AIA Honor Award for the design of the Nosler House, which continues to appear in numerous publications.

The design is only half of the story. Without the dedicated involvement of general contractor Greg Marrone as well as his staff, the outcome could have been significantly different. Greg and his chief estimator, Don Wallace, joined the team early in the design process, and even with a substantial budget, helped keep the project within reach. They also made significant contributions to the design, facilitating the actual production of the home's numerous unique features.

For a residential project, it is most unusual to have a highly qualified superintendent assigned full-time to be overseeing every detail. As mentioned, Steve Gonzales exceeded all expectations—from his marvelous interactions with both Kay and myself, to his very talented ability to guide the creation of numerous challenging details.

Creating a book that captures the essence of the project from beginning to end is no small achievement. The original idea was forcefully promoted by William Peters, the landscape architect whom we brought onto the project midway through the design phase. His gardens on all four sides of the house were so thoughtfully attuned to the expanses of glass and provided such a complement to the Thodos design.

Following William's initial writing efforts, Erik and I began in earnest to produce a book that would memorialize the project. Very early in that process Jerry Takigawa, a noted book designer with a nearby office in Monterey, joined the team with the principal task of creating a memorable book from the dozens of photos and completed writings. Finally, on Jerry's recommendation, we added a very talented editor, Eric Edward Brown, to the team.

—Peter Nosler, April 2019

APPENDIX

Approaching the glow of the main entry along the oblique entrance pathway and the striking street-facing view of the home at dusk.

Pages 4–5

The inviting glass-block entrance portico leading to the spine hall.

Having entered the front door, this is the view down the entire length of the sky-lit spine hall with the rear door portal to the back garden in the distance.

Pages 6–7

View of the living room with its floor-to-ceiling, undulating glass wall.

View looking back at the front door and the adjoining living room.

Pages 8–9

The glass enclosed stairway to the lower level from the atrium.

View climbing back up the stairway with the extruded, stepped exterior forms beyond the glass enclosure.

Pages 10–11

View across the master bedroom to the garden beyond.

View looking back at the rear door portal with its protective glass canopy.

Pages 12–13

The Nosler House from the street. The translucent Italian glass block both lets in light and ensures privacy, while providing another wonderful material texture for the critical street elevation.

Pages 66–67

The front door beckons you into the wide "hall room." The red doorframe, cantilevered off the floor, is surrounded by glass.

Top left: *Here is an ultra-modern house situated in a redwood grove. The "soft" decomposed granite walk and driveway help the more "edgy" architectural style fit into its natural setting.*

Bottom left: *The floor-to-ceiling glass of the living room wraps around the vertically cantilevered, red steel door portal: the scale of the individual expressed through architecture. The artisan-crafted stone wall provides a border to the living room space while graciously leading you down the side yard.*

Pages 68–69

The living room becomes extra-spacious as it flows into the hallway. Trees and plants wrap around the rather narrow city lot, creating a sense of isolation even though located on a traditional residential street.

The bridge table in the living room, framed by greenery that surrounds it via the transparency and translucency of the living room glazing.

Pages 70–71

The delightful wide hallway with its glass roof heading towards the front door. The special Italian glass block is an abundant source of light yet provides privacy from the street.

The Italian glass block was one of the superb discoveries made by architect John Thodos.

Pages 72–73

View from the opening to the dining room across from the gracious hall. The layering of foreground (hall and artwork), middle ground (living room sitting area with glass behind) and background (artisan stone wall with hedge of the side yard garden) can be appreciated. Also notice the fine craftmanship and scale of the flush white-oak baseboard.

The living room looking out into the hallway: the perfect spot for Robert Goodnough's large painting, "Four Clusters."

Pages 74–75

One of several "niches" that architect John Thodos used to separate the functional spaces attached to the hallway spine—thereby creating an opportunity for glazing a third wall into the living room on the right, and another window onto the hallway.

The northern side door, the principal entry for the home's residents. The dining room and kitchen hide behind the large Japanese maple on the right. A traditional house might have two or three wall and roof surfaces, while here there are at least nine.

Pages 76–77

The kitchen side door as seen up close. So many surfaces!

Peter and Kay fell in love with having a lower kitchen table when they visited friends in Italy. It was ideal for Kay in a wheelchair but is far more inviting for most any kitchen, especially with natural light coming in on all sides of the room.

Pages 78–79

From the driveway looking toward the glass atrium, with the kitchen and dining room to the left. Note the giant redwood so close to the house, with several more in the distance.

The U-shaped stairs to the lower level. It required two concrete pours to get this right. Notice the curved wall with the hint of the vertical siding captured in the concrete.

Pages 80–81

Emerging up the stairs from the lower level to the glass atrium, with the curved glass wall and glass ceiling supported by a light-steel framing system.

The view from the "glass room" looking towards the front door, with the hallway's unusual width clearly visible. At right is an isolated entrance to the elevator, with stairs to the lower level on the left.

Pages 82–83

View from Peter's office. The use of floor-to-ceiling glass allows this relatively small space to feel like it's part of the garden beyond, with the beautiful artisan stone wall extending across.

The west end of the spine/hall looking towards the front—full of art and light.

Pages 84–85

A small niche in the spine/hall for a whimsical piece of art.

The master bath shower was dubbed the "drive-in shower," with no curbs or obstruction. The sliding glass door seals the shower and is fully equipped with grab bars.

Right: The master bathroom, looking into the master bedroom and the backyard garden beyond. The vanities are located against the wall of the hall, which doesn't extend to the ceiling, thereby allowing natural light from the spine skylight to be "stolen" into the room.

Pages 86–87

View of the bay window in Kay's studio looking out towards the garden.

From the backyard garden looking into the quilting studio.

Pages 88–89

The backyard with the quilting studio at left and the master bedroom at right. This small yard is a contemplative space with ample greenery and a gurgling fountain.

Pages 90–91

The back door, framed in red steel with glass overhang, and its twin in the distance.

The front door as seen up close, focusing on the lovely entry vestibule with the spacious hallway beyond.

Pages 92–93

The house in the forest. The living room on the left, then the inviting entry, with the dining room on the right. An eight-year-old trick-or-treater at the front door once said: "Boy, this is the coolest house!"

Pages 94–95